A Picture Book of
Paul Revere

David A. Adler

illustrated by John & Alexandra Wallner

Holiday House/New York

Others books in David A. Adler's *Picture Book Biography* series

A Picture Book of George Washington

A Picture Book of Abraham Lincoln

A Picture Book of Martin Luther King, Jr.

A Picture Book of Thomas Jefferson

A Picture Book of Benjamin Franklin

A Picture Book of Helen Keller

A Picture Book of Eleanor Roosevelt

A Picture Book of Christopher Columbus

A Picture Book of John F. Kennedy

A Picture Book of Simón Bolívar

A Picture Book of Harriet Tubman

A Picture Book of Florence Nightingale

A Picture Book of Jesse Owens

A Picture Book of Anne Frank

A Picture Book of Frederick Douglass

A Picture Book of Sitting Bull

A Picture Book of Rosa Parks

A Picture Book of Robert E. Lee

A Picture Book of Sojourner Truth

A Picture Book of Jackie Robinson

Library of Congress Cataloging-in-Publication Data
Adler, David A.
A picture book of Paul Revere / David A. Adler ; illustrated by
John & Alexandra Wallner.
p.   cm.
ISBN 0-8234-1144-3
1. Revere, Paul, 1735–1818—Juvenile literature.   2. Statesmen—
Massachusetts—Biography—Juvenile literature.   3. Massachusetts—
Biography—Juvenile literature.   4. Massachusetts—History—
Revolution, 1775–1783—Juvenile literature.   I. Wallner, John C.
II. Wallner, Alexandra.   III. Title.
F69.R43A35   1995   94-9783   CIP   AC
973.3'311'092—dc20
[B]
ISBN 0-8234-1294-6 (pbk.)

Paul Revere was born in a small, crowded house on Fish Street near the edge of Boston Harbor. He was the son of Paul and Deborah Revere, the second of their nine children. He was born on New Year's Day, 1735.

Paul learned his ABCs at an "infant school" where he also learned to say "please" and "thank you" and other rules of good manners. Then, when he was seven or eight, he went to North Writing, an all-boys' school. There he learned to read, write, and do basic arithmetic.

At thirteen Paul Revere left school to work in his father's shop. His father was a silversmith.

When Paul was fifteen he and six other boys formed a society to ring the eight large bells in the steeple of Christ Church. The bells were said to have the sweetest sound of any in the American colonies.

Paul Revere's father died in 1754. Paul was nineteen. Since he was the oldest son, it was his job to support his mother, sisters, and brothers. He worked in his father's silversmith shop with his younger brother Thomas.

During Paul's childhood, Massachusetts was one of the thirteen American colonies controlled by Great Britain. To the north and west was territory controlled by France. Beginning in 1689, there were battles along the borders between the British and French called the French and Indian Wars. Native Americans fought for both sides.

In February 1756, Paul Revere joined a Massachusetts regiment to fight the French. They marched to Fort William Henry at Lake George, New York.

Paul Revere's regiment fought minor battles and had no real victories. More soldiers died from disease than from fighting. In November 1756, the surviving soldiers, including Paul Revere, were sent home.

Paul went back to work in his shop. He was an excellent silver-smith and was busy six days a week making silver teapots, punch bowls, earrings, shoe buckles, clock faces, baby rattles, whistles, dog collars, and even a chain for someone's pet squirrel. On Sundays he went to church.

It was in church that Paul met Sara Orne. During the minister's sermons, Paul kept watching her. Then he courted Sara, and they married in August 1757.

Sara moved into the house on Fish Street with Paul's family. The small house became even more crowded as Paul and Sara began having children. They had eight altogether, one born just about every other year beginning in 1758.

Two of the children died young, including Isanna, the youngest, who died at nine months. Perhaps it was a difficult delivery because five months after Isanna was born, Sara died.

One summer evening, shortly after his wife died, Paul met Rachel Walker. He was hurrying home to care for his children, and Rachel came to help.

Rachel Walker was a kind, capable woman. Paul called her his "Dear Girl." They married on September 23, 1773, and they, too, had eight children. Three of the children died young.

With so many children, Paul Revere had to be sure he could always earn a living. Only wealthy people could afford to buy things made of silver, so Paul learned other trades. He worked as a goldsmith. He learned to clean real teeth and make false ones. He engraved copper plates and printed pictures and business cards, fixed umbrellas, and made eyeglasses.

Paul Revere was busy with his work and family. Beginning in the 1760s he busied himself with politics, too. Paul joined the Sons of Liberty, a society of Americans who were against British rule in the colonies.

By 1763, the war with France had ended, but there were still British soldiers in the colonies. In March 1765, to pay for the soldiers, the British Parliament passed the Stamp Act. It was a tax on newspapers and other printed matter.

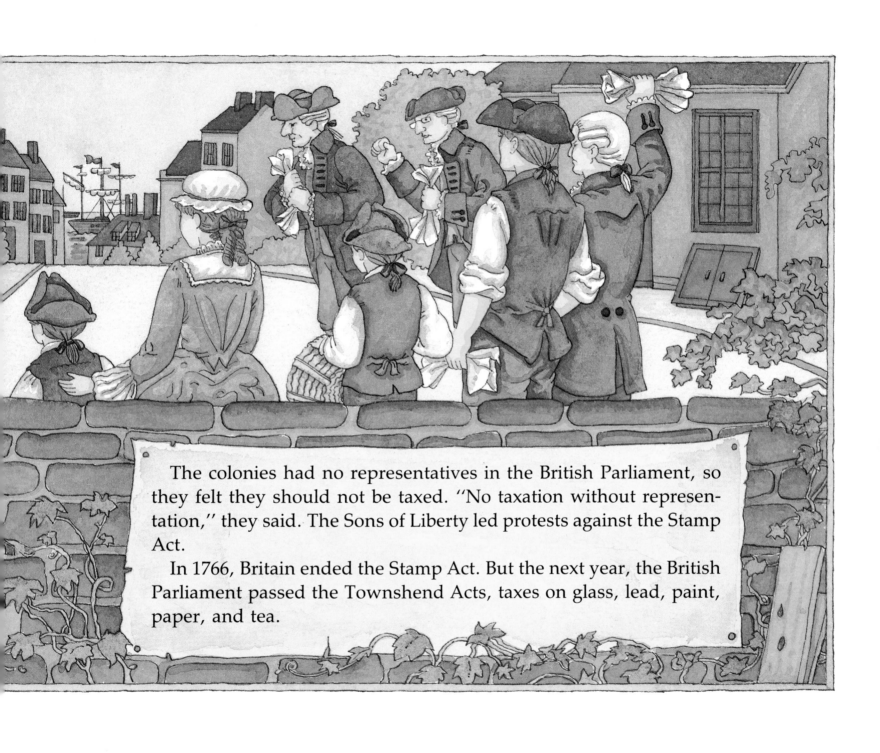

The colonies had no representatives in the British Parliament, so they felt they should not be taxed. "No taxation without representation," they said. The Sons of Liberty led protests against the Stamp Act.

In 1766, Britain ended the Stamp Act. But the next year, the British Parliament passed the Townshend Acts, taxes on glass, lead, paint, paper, and tea.

On March 5, 1770, Britain ended those taxes, too, all except for the tax on tea. On that same day, on King Street in Boston, there was a fight with British soldiers.

A group of colonists threw snowballs, ice, wood, and coal at them. They shouted at the soldiers and called them "lobsters" and "bloody backs" because of their red uniforms.

There was a fight and some soldiers fired their guns. Five colonists, four men, and one boy were killed in what was later called the "Boston Massacre."

Paul Revere made an engraving of the massacre with the soldiers all in a line firing their guns at peaceful citizens. It was certainly not a true picture of what happened, but Paul Revere wanted to stir up hatred for the British. And he did.

Late in 1773, three British ships loaded with tea sailed into Boston Harbor. Many of the people of Boston wouldn't pay the tax and they wouldn't drink the tea.

On December 16, 1773, a large group of Bostonians disguised themselves as Native Americans. They divided into three groups, one led by Paul Revere, and boarded the ships. They broke open the 342 chests of tea and dumped them in the water.

On May 10, 1774, five thousand British soldiers arrived in Boston to close the harbor. It would remain closed until the people of Boston agreed to pay for the tea.

They never did.

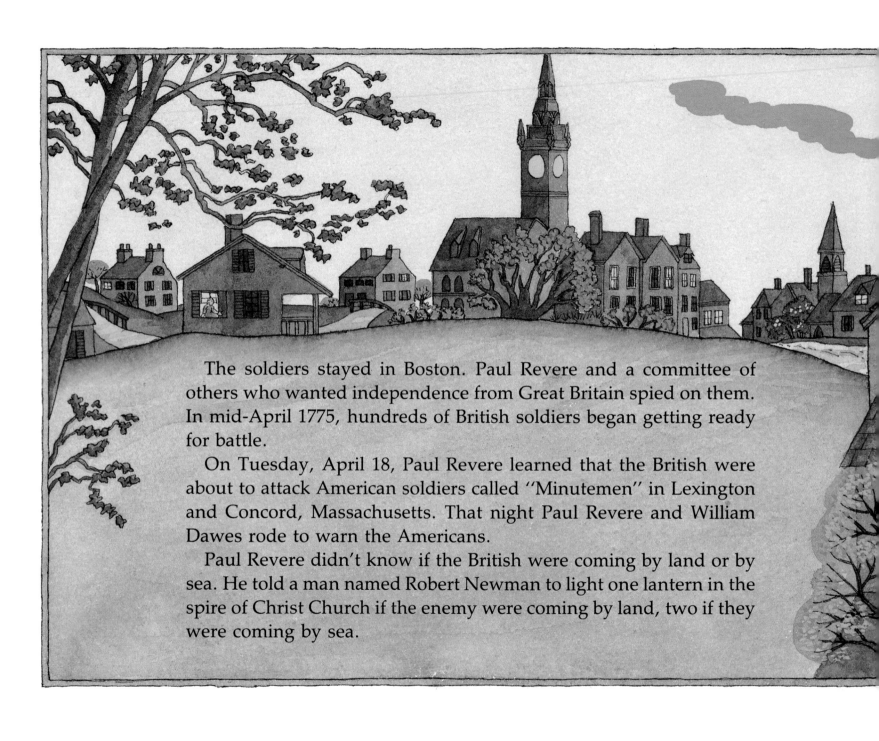

The soldiers stayed in Boston. Paul Revere and a committee of others who wanted independence from Great Britain spied on them. In mid-April 1775, hundreds of British soldiers began getting ready for battle.

On Tuesday, April 18, Paul Revere learned that the British were about to attack American soldiers called "Minutemen" in Lexington and Concord, Massachusetts. That night Paul Revere and William Dawes rode to warn the Americans.

Paul Revere didn't know if the British were coming by land or by sea. He told a man named Robert Newman to light one lantern in the spire of Christ Church if the enemy were coming by land, two if they were coming by sea.

Paul Revere left Boston by crossing the Charles River. William Dawes left through the town gate. They met at Lexington and warned their countrymen there.

Samuel Prescott joined them. Then, on their way to Concord, Paul Revere was caught by British officers. The British took away his horse, but they didn't harm him. William Dawes rode off in such a hurry that he fell off his horse. Only Samuel Prescott got through to warn the Americans in Concord.

Early the next morning at Lexington, shots were fired. The fight for the independence of the American colonies, the Revolutionary War, had begun.

On July 4, 1776, representatives of the thirteen colonies at the Second Continental Congress in Philadelphia approved the Declaration of Independence. It declared that the thirteen colonies were free and independent states, no longer ruled by the British king or Parliament.

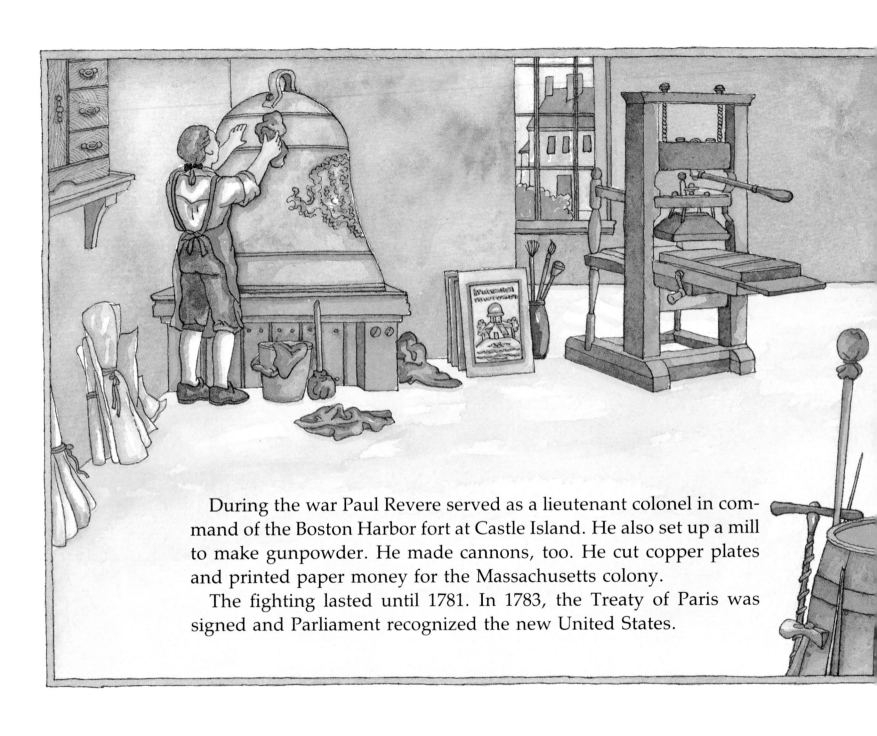

During the war Paul Revere served as a lieutenant colonel in command of the Boston Harbor fort at Castle Island. He also set up a mill to make gunpowder. He made cannons, too. He cut copper plates and printed paper money for the Massachusetts colony.

The fighting lasted until 1781. In 1783, the Treaty of Paris was signed and Parliament recognized the new United States.

After the war, Paul Revere went back to work as a silversmith. He made large bells to hang in church steeples. He sold playing cards, sealing wax, wallpaper, and cloth. He worked in copper, too, making parts for ships, and set up a rolling mill to make copper sheets to cover the bottom of American warships.

As Paul Revere grew older, he was surrounded by his grandchildren, and then his great-grandchildren. He told them often of his adventures before and during the American Revolution.

Paul Revere died on May 10, 1818, after a long illness. He had many talents, but mostly he is remembered as an American patriot who helped his country win its independence.

AUTHOR'S NOTE

The Christ Church is now known as the Old North Church.

Paul Revere made many rides to help American patriots before and during the War of Independence. Immediately following the Boston Tea Party, he rode to New York and Philadelphia to tell about what the people of Boston had done. When Boston Harbor was closed, Paul Revere rode again to inform Americans in New York and Philadelphia. Beginning in 1772, the Sons of Liberty formed Committees of Correspondence in different towns and colonies to send each other news about their struggles with the British. Paul Revere often rode carrying letters for the committees. He also rode carrying letters for the Committees of Safety, which helped inform and govern the colonies during the Revolutionary War.

Some of Paul Revere's lasting fame is due to "Paul Revere's Ride," a ballad written by Henry Wadsworth Longfellow (1807–1882).

IMPORTANT DATES

1735   Born in Boston, Massachusetts, on January 1.

1748   Began work as an apprentice in his father's silversmith shop.

1754   Father, Apollos Rivioire (in the 1720s he renamed himself Paul Revere), died on July 22. Paul took over the shop.

1756   Joined a Massachusetts regiment on February 18 and was made a second lieutenant in the artillery group.

1757   Married Sara Orne in August.

1770   Made an engraving of the Boston Massacre.

1773   Wife Sara died on May 3.

1773   Married Rachel Walker on September 23.

1773   Participated in Boston Tea Party on December 16.

1775   At night, on April 18, he rode to Lexington, Massachusetts, to deliver the news that the British were coming.

1776   The Declaration of Independence was adopted by the Second Continental Congress on July 4.

1813   Wife Rachel died on June 26.

1818   Died on May 10 in Boston, Massachusetts.